Honk, Honk, Goose!

Canada Geese Start a Family

April Pulley Sayre • illustrated by Huy Voun Lee

Henry Holt and Company

New York

Honk, hee-honk, honk!
In chilly mid-March, a male goose called and chased.
He chased squirrels. *Honk!*
Ducks. *Honk!*
Geese. *Honk, hee-honk, honk!*

He chased away all except a female goose.

He and she spent all their time together.

Dabble, dip, they paddled in the pond. Pluck, pull, they fed on plants. Stretch, curve, their necks danced. Then they mated. *Splash, splash,* they took baths.

Inside the female goose, eggs began to form. It was time to make a nest.

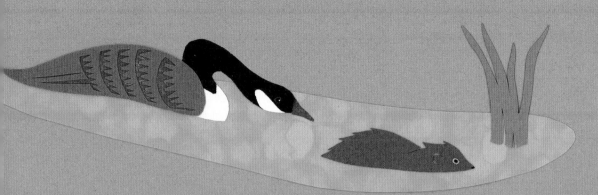

Honk, hee-honk!
The male chased
away a muskrat.

Honk! He snapped at
a snapping turtle.

Honk, hee-honk, honk!
He rushed at an opossum.

The female goose stacked sticks and grasses. She plucked soft feathers from her breast and used them to line the nest.

Then she started laying eggs—one each day. One. One. One. One. One.

On the fifth day, when the geese were feeding, a raccoon rolled an egg out of the nest. *Crack!*

Honk, hee-honk, honk! Hisssssssssssss! the male goose called.

Flap, flap. He lunged. The raccoon ran. But one egg was already broken.

The next day the female laid another. . . and the next day, she laid the last.

All the eggs were laid, so she sat on them to warm them. Now and then, she stood and turned the eggs. The male goose floated nearby.

Honk!
He honked at a kingfisher.

Honk! at a skunk.

Honk, hee-honk, honk!
He chased off a heron.

Early each morning and evening, the female goose took breaks to bathe and eat. Under their goose-down blanket, the eggs stayed warm until she returned.

For twenty-eight days, the mother goose sat on the eggs. Then, she heard a sound.

Crack!

Crick!

Peep!

The chicks were hatching!
First one. Then two at once.

Then suddenly, three!
Six wet chicks dried in
the sun.

The male goose stood guard.
Honk! he honked at the squirrels.
Honk! at the ducks.

Honk, hee-honk, honk!
at neighboring geese.

The day after the chicks hatched, the father and mother took a stroll. Twelve wobbly goose legs followed.

The parents slid into the water. The chicks followed.

Plop!

Plop!

Plop! Plop!

Plop! Plop!

Dabble, dip, they paddled. Pluck, pull, they fed on plants.

The mother goose walked up the muddy bank
and settled down to rest.

Scratch, slip, slip, the tired chicks climbed.
Peep, peep, peep! They scrambled for places
under her wings.

Peep! Yawn. *Peep!* Yawn. Eyelids drooped.
Soon, the chicks were asleep. Every goose
slept except . . .

. . . the father goose, who stood guard.
He stayed alert, ready to chase away danger.

Honk, hee-honk, honk!
Hissssssss!

~Canada Goose Families~

Canada geese live not only in Canada but across almost all of the United States. In spring, geese establish nesting sites. The male defends his site, honking and hissing loudly, bobbing his neck, and chasing off other animals, including other geese. Male and female Canada geese mate for life. If one mate dies, the surviving goose may look for another mate.

Geese nest on slightly raised areas near water. A shoreline, small island, or muskrat lodge will do. Canada geese often nest on the same site each year. The female builds a bowl of dry grasses, sticks, and moss. She lines it with down from her breast. These downy feathers are similar to those used in comforters and coats. (The feathers in coats and comforters are from domestic, or farm-raised, geese.) These feathers are good insulation and help keep the eggs warm when the female goose is incubating them or when she leaves the nest in order to bathe and eat.

Female Canada geese usually lay between four and seven eggs. The female incubates the eggs for 25 to 28 days. Two days before the chicks hatch, they begin making tapping, clicking noises, which can be heard through the shell. Then they hatch, pushing out of their shells.

It's not uncommon for only three or four chicks from a wild nest to survive. Some nests are flooded by rising river waters. Predators, such as skunks, dogs, foxes, gulls, ravens, bears, snapping turtles, and raccoons, may eat eggs or chicks. The chicks that do survive grow quickly. Unlike many other baby birds, Canada goose chicks can feed, walk, and swim within a day after hatching.

Canada geese feed on leaves, seeds, berries, insects, and sometimes small fish. They can sleep while standing, sitting, or floating. Some adult geese sleep while paddling one foot so they swim in a circle! When asleep, their body quiets and their breathing slows. But they may keep one eye, or even both eyes, open.

Soon after hatching, each young chick grows flight feathers. The young chicks strengthen their wing muscles by flapping and running. Six to nine weeks after hatching, the young geese take their first flights. Yet they stay with their parents for an entire year. Goose families migrate together.

~Migrating Geese and Resident Geese~

A hundred years ago, many people feared they would never see or hear geese again. Canada geese had disappeared entirely from some parts of the northern United States and Canada. So people took action to help the birds. They bred Canada geese. They released these geese at lakes and ponds. The population of Canada geese grew.

These released geese did not migrate long distances as their wild ancestors had. They settled in to live in city parks and golf courses. These places have low grass near ponds—the kind of habitat Canada geese prefer. Some ponds, lakes, and golf courses now have huge flocks of these "resident" geese.

The droppings of a few geese can fertilize a lawn and make it grow well. But large flocks that remain in a small area can produce enough droppings to kill off lawns, contaminate the water, and make an area less desirable for golfers or picnickers. So some landowners try to discourage the geese from staying on their land.

Wild migrating flocks of geese still exist and in some areas are doing well. They breed in the tundra and forests of Canada, Alaska, and Greenland. They spend the winter in the southeastern United States and northern Mexico. Wild geese have not increased in number as much as resident geese. In some years, the wild goose population has sharply decreased, while in other years the population has increased. Currently, the wild goose population is doing well. People can continue to enjoy a favorite sign of fall and spring—the sight of V-shaped flocks of geese in the air.

~Big Geese, Little Geese~

Adult Canada geese vary in size, neck length, coloration, and call. Recently the American Ornithological Union officially divided Canada geese into two species. The larger-bodied geese are now Canada geese (*Branta canadensis*), and the smaller-bodied geese are Cackling geese (*Branta hutchinsii*). Both species have the kind of family life described in this book.

~Young Scientists!~

Scientists have never done a long-term study of goose behavior. Perhaps you will be the first one to do this work. Watching geese is a great way to learn about bird behavior and practice your scientific observation skills.

For my niece Virginia,
who sees with her heart.
Keep on singing!
—A. P. S.

~Author's Note~ To add to my personal observations of geese, I consulted a library of scientific papers and general reference books, such as Kenn Kaufman's *Lives of North American Birds* (Boston: Houghton Mifflin, 1996) and David Allen Sibley's *The Sibley Guide to Birds* (New York: Alfred A. Knopf, 1996). Many Web sites about geese were confusing or misleading. The deepest, most reliable information on birds, particularly Canada geese, was available in the 18,000-page, 18-volume *Birds of North America*, which is available online at http://bna.birds.cornell.edu for a small fee.

My thanks to Tom Mowbray for his scientific review.

Henry Holt and Company, LLC
Publishers since 1866
175 Fifth Avenue
New York, New York 10010
www.HenryHoltKids.com

Library of Congress Cataloging-in-Publication Data
Sayre, April Pulley.
Honk, honk, goose! : Canada geese start a family / April Pulley Sayre ;
illustrated by Huy Voun Lee.—1st ed.
p.   cm.
ISBN-13: 978-0-8050-7103-0 / ISBN-10: 0-8050-7103-2
1. Canada goose—Juvenile literature. I. Lee, Huy Voun, ill. II. Title.
QL696.A52S39 2009   598.4′178—dc22   2008013423

First Edition—2009 / Designed by Elynn Cohen
The artist used cut-paper collage to create the illustrations for this book.
Printed in China on acid-free paper. ∞

10 9 8 7 6 5 4 3 2 1